A souvenir guide

Trengwainton Garden
Cornwall

Katherine Lambert

🌳 **National Trust**

GW00692134

A very warm welcome to Trengwainton

There has been a house here for centuries and many generations have left their imprint on the garden, from the flamboyant and eccentric Sir Rose Price to the six generations of my family that have lived here to date. However, it was my grandfather, Lieutenant Colonel Sir Edward Bolitho, whom we have to thank for transforming Trengwainton into one of the great gardens of Cornwall.

Inheriting the property from his uncle, he also inherited an outstanding head gardener and propagator in Alfred Creek, and together they set about transforming the garden. Plant material and advice from his Cornish garden friends, and seed from Frank Kingdon-Ward's expeditions to Upper Burma provided the backbone of the garden in the 1920s and 1930s.

Much change has happened since then, with new plantings naturally succeeding the old, but also being necessary due to the vagaries of disease and weather. However, a great number of the original plants remain in this fine woodland garden.

In 1961, approaching his 80th birthday and wanting to preserve it for future generations at a time of crippling taxation, Sir Edward gave the garden to the National Trust, along with neighbouring property and a substantial financial endowment. My family continue to live in the house and remain closely involved with the running of the garden, alongside the excellent team of staff and volunteers.

I really hope you have a great visit and that you will come again many times. You must see the camellias and incredible flowering magnolias of early spring. These are followed by the equally dramatic rhododendrons, and then summer brings the stream area into full flower before late summer and autumn, when the hydrangeas keep the colours going, matching the wonderful Cornish light. The recently restored Kitchen Garden provides a very enjoyable contrast throughout the year. Enjoy them all!

Edward Bolitho

Opposite, far right
A tree fern (*Dicksonia antarctica*) unfurling in June

Right The depth and variety of the planting at Trengwainton bring visitors back time and again

Above Edward and Alexandra Bolitho

The History of Trengwainton

To fully appreciate what Trengwainton has to offer today, we must first delve a little deeper into the past – to find out how and where this unique kaleidoscope of plants originated, and to learn more about the visionary collectors and gardeners who made the garden's reputation.

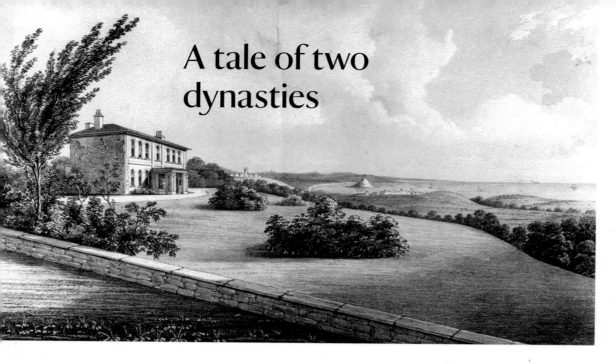

A tale of two dynasties

Trengwainton is a garden with an intriguing history, a unique layout, and a rich and rare diversity of plants. Two very different families stamped their mark on it over two centuries, but they complement each other in a most fascinating way. The garden today is a reflection of them both.

Although date stones record late-medieval and Tudor houses at Trengwainton, it was not until 1817 that it was transformed, by an exotic newcomer, into a proper country seat. Sir Rose Price had roots in Penzance, but his wealth came from the sugar plantations that his family had owned in Jamaica for 150 years.

As Price re-established himself in the county of his birth, his ambitions were as high as his pockets were deep, and he set out to create for himself, his Irish wife and 14 children a home on the grandest scale. A broad new drive, flanked by beech, ash and sycamore, swept from an ornamental Doric entrance lodge up to the house, which was luxuriously modernised inside and given a handsome Regency facelift. A 71-acre complex of plantations and shrubberies grounded the house in its setting, a broad terrace walk drew attention to the magnificent view over Mount's Bay to St Michael's Mount and the Lizard Peninsula, and a walled kitchen garden of revolutionary design was carved out of a four-acre field.

While Price's mansion and grounds were taking shape, the Bolithos – the old Cornish family who make up the other half of Trengwainton's story – had been established as merchants since the early 18th century. By the 19th century their tentacles spread to embrace tanning and ship-owning, tin smelting and tin mining, fishing and farming, and, most importantly, banking.

In August 1833, the Slavery Abolition Act cut the ground from under the feet of Price and his fellow plantation owners. Shortly after his death in 1834, the estate was disposed of at auction, paving the way for the second dynasty.

Tin mining in Cornwall

In the 18th and 19th centuries, Cornishmen in the tin-mining belt in the southern half of the county – from Perranporth to Penzance – were profiting from seemingly inexhaustible deposits of mineral ore embedded in the granite soil.

Engineers of genius and versatility, including Thomas Newcomen and Richard Trevithick, invented the hundreds of steam engines needed to pump water out of the deep mine shafts. In Hayle, Camborne and Perranarworthal, the owners of foundries built and serviced pumping engines, man engines, drills, steam winches and all the other accoutrements of the industry for the local smelting firms to use. At the top of the heap was a new breed of industrialist, families like the Bolithos of Trengwainton and Trewidden: mercantile adventurers, willing and usually able to switch their funds as one trading door closed and another opened.

But neither the invention nor the money-making would have been possible without the proud and doggedly courageous men who worked the vertical shafts, some 1,800 feet deep, others running 200 feet under and over a mile

Left Towanroath Shaft engine house, once containing a beam engine used to pump water from Wheal Coates mine, now a romantic ruin

Below left Richard Trevithick's water wheel at Cook's Kitchen mine

Below Man engines were used to transport miners and operated like a moving ladder

out to sea. *Tin,* a novel written in 1888 which was made into a film starring Jenny Agutter in 2015, vividly describes the regular perils: foul air, slippery ladders, falling ground, 'houses of water' and explosions of dynamite and gunpowder. Thomas Robins Bolitho was on the committee of the Levant Mining Company (formed in 1820) during the appalling disaster of 1919, when a man engine broke and a 'human pillar' coming off shift crashed into the shaft at the mine near St Just and 31 men were lost.

At the height of production in the 19th century, the county was the world leader in tin, but the economic scene was always shifting, usually downwards. Prices fell at the end of the Napoleonic Wars and again in the 1840s, as cheaper imports arrived from Australia, Bolivia and Malaya; there was a brief boom in the early 1870s and a big slump in the 1890s. The last mine, South Crofty, closed in 1998, and a county long defined by smoke, grime and noise, by shafts, engine houses and railways, by workers' cottages, overseers' houses and bankers' mansions was gradually transformed into a lunar landscape. Today, however, it has reinvented itself as a World Heritage Site and a tourist draw. You just can't keep Kernow down.

The Bolithos

The 30 years that followed Price's death marked the only time that the future of Trengwainton hung in the balance. It was in a sad state in 1867, when Thomas Simon Bolitho stepped in to buy the 900 acres on offer, including the mansion and its garden, plantations, farms and arable land.

A keen agriculturist, he made a major start to renovating the property, but it was his son, Thomas Robins Bolitho, inheriting 20 years later, who set about enlarging and remodelling the house, improving the grounds and building a new and wider carriage drive. In fact, he was carrying on where Price had left off, with Trengwainton again used as the marker for the family's success.

The Bolithos occupied high status in the county. Successive generations filled one or more of the county positions: as Mayor, County Councillor, Justice of the Peace, High Sherriff and Lord Lieutenant. Thomas Simon Bolitho also served as Deputy Warden of the Stannaries, the ancient but extant judicial and military court peculiar to Cornwall.

Exciting imports

It was Thomas Robins Bolitho's successor, his 43-year-old nephew Lieutenant Colonel E. H. W. Bolitho of the Royal Field Artillery, who brought about Trengwainton's second great renaissance after 1925. With advice from his cousins, J. C. and P. D. Williams, who had laid out famous gardens at Caerhays and Lanarth, and another gardening neighbour, Canon A. T. Boscawen of Ludgvan, he planted pleasure grounds and opened up the stream beside the drive. Had he not then been bitten by the plant-collecting bug, and had he not inherited in Alfred Creek a head gardener with legendarily green fingers, Trengwainton's amazing collection of species rhododendrons, buttressed by a wealth of tender ornamentals, would not have existed. The wheel had turned full circle: Sir Rose Price came from an exotic climate, E. H. W. Bolitho imported it.

First flowerings

The gardening fraternity evidently took the newcomer to their hearts, with George Johnstone of Trewithen and Lawrence Johnston of Hidcote Manor in Gloucestershire offering him some of the booty gathered by Frank Kingdon-Ward during his 1927–28 expedition to north-east Assam and the Mishmi Hills of upper Burma. E. H. W. Bolitho was to later write about this contribution: 'In fact, the whole garden is founded on this one sending.'

The precious seeds were propagated by Creek and distributed in carefully selected and sheltered parts of the garden. Some of the rhododendrons from the expedition flowered at Trengwainton for the first time in Britain, and the southern half of Price's walled garden started to bloom with the tenderest species of rhododendrons and other marginally hardy ornamental plants.

New management

E. H. W. Bolitho professed himself really only interested in the big picture, claiming that he only gardened 'above the waist'. Fortunately for today's visitors, the next two generations provided the last missing link in the garden we see today.

His son, Major Simon (1969–91), made the banks and background of the stream into a marvellous ribbon of spring and summer colour. The plantings in front of the house have been revived and expanded by the present head of the family, Colonel Edward, and the Terrace has been furnished by the National Trust (who acquired the garden in 1961) with a broad herbaceous border. Meanwhile, the replacement avenues of evergreen oaks, almost all uprooted in the great storm of 1990, grow tall.

History, structure, horticulture – Trengwainton has it all.

Above Thomas Simon Bolitho and his wife Elizabeth

Left The Bolitho coat of arms

Right The Lower Drive in the 19th century

Far right E. H. W. Bolitho and his wife Agnes; in 1953 he became Sir Edward

The plant hunters

Above *Charles II Presented with a Pineapple;* by Hendrik Danckerts, 1677

In 1677 Dutch artist Hendrik Danckerts recorded a memorable horticultural event: the presentation to Charles II of the first pineapple to be grown in the British Isles. In 2000 the newspapers were mesmerised by the kidnapping of an orchid-seeking botanist, Tom Hart Dyke, in hostile territory between Panama and Colombia. During the three and more centuries in between, the exploits of the plant hunters have become the stuff of legend.

Many of these intrepid men – Sir Joseph Banks, David Douglas, Sir Joseph Hooker, Robert Fortune, Ernest 'Chinese' Wilson – were British, and each one carved out his own small fiefdom in different parts of the globe, from the Americas to Australasia, South Africa to South-East Asia, China to the Himalayas. George Forrest (1873–1932) and Frank Kingdon-Ward (1885–1958), perhaps the last two of the golden age of plant hunting, overlapped not only in time but also, to Forrest's annoyance, in place (north-west Yunnan).

Horticultural huntsmen

The plant hunters came from all parts of the country and all walks of life, but what they had in common was exceptional courage, determination, loyalty to sponsors and devotion to purpose. As related calmly and often humorously in their letters and books, the dangers were very real, ranging from being impaled on spikes, falling into bear pits and being hunted down by murderous gangs of llamas!

But the rewards were very tangible – imagine the first public sighting of the giant Amazonian water-lily, *Victoria regia*, discovered by Robert Schomburgk during his 1835–44 expedition to Guyana and presented to the Duke of Devonshire at Chatsworth. Here, Joseph Paxton designed an airy glasshouse for it and at its unveiling posed his young daughter Annie in the centre of one of the huge saucer-shaped leaves.

As well as having a pervasive and permanent effect on British gardening, their introductions also influenced art and architecture, from Marianne North's dramatic gallery of plant portraits at Kew to the horticultural encrustations of the Royal Pavilion in Brighton.

Now available in Cornwall

Kingdon-Ward introductions included *Meconopsis betonicifolia, Primula florindae* (named after his first wife), and from the 1927–8 expedition, *Rhododendron macabeanum, R. elliottii, R. taggianum, R. concatenans* and many other species never before bred in Britain.

They grow here among garden favourites introduced into the UK by earlier plant hunters: *Phormium tenax* by Banks; *Zantedeschia aethiopica* by Charles Masson; *Pinus radiata* by Douglas; *Rhododendron falconeri* and *R. thomsonii* by Hooker; *Cryptomeria japonica* and *Rhododendron fortunei* by Fortune; *Cornus kousa* var. *chinensis* by Wilson; and *R. sinogrande, R. griersonianum, Camellia reticulata, C. saluenensis* and *Magnolia campbellii* ssp. *mollicomata* by Forrest. As you make your own expedition round the garden, do seek them out.

Left Joseph Banks by Sir Joshua Reynolds

Below left One of the greatest plant hunters of his or any other age, Sir Joseph Dalton Hooker

Below right Frank Kingdon-Ward

An award-winning garden

Trengwainton was graded II* by English Heritage in 2002. It was, however, recognised as a garden of exceptional merit long before that. The Bolithos set great store by exhibiting at Royal Horticultural Society and local shows, and over the years the garden has accumulated a plethora of prizes and accolades.

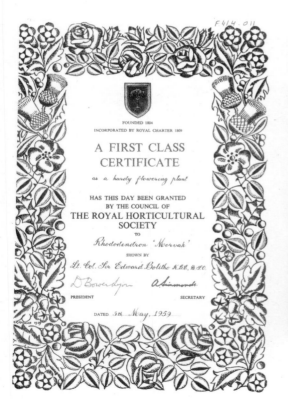

FOUNDED 1804
INCORPORATED BY ROYAL CHARTER 1809

A FIRST CLASS CERTIFICATE

as a hardy flowering plant

HAS THIS DAY BEEN GRANTED
BY THE COUNCIL OF
THE ROYAL HORTICULTURAL
SOCIETY
TO
Rhododendron 'Morvah'

SHOWN BY
Lt. Col. Sir Edward Bolitho K.B.E. D.S.O.

PRESIDENT   SECRETARY

DATED 5th May, 1959

Left Award of Merit for
Rhododendron 'Morvah',
22 May 1956

Left The walls and ceiling of the Bothy are covered with decades' worth of prize certificates

Right *Rhododendron macabeanum*

Below Award of Merit for *R. macabeanum*, 23 March 1937

Above First Class Certificate for *R.* 'Fusilier', 19 May 1942

Left *R.* 'Fusilier'

A Tour of the Garden

Trengwainton's 29 acres stand 390 feet above sea level at their highest point. They lie only 36 miles from Tresco on the Isles of Scilly, but the very different conditions enable plantings that are 'lush exotic' rather than exclusively tropical. An exceptionally long growing and flowering season means a tour of Trengwainton can be taken from spring through to autumn.

Right **The Lower Drive leads you through jewelled clusters of rhododendrons under towering trees**

Far right, above
Rhododendron loderi

Far right, below
Wollemia nobilis

The Lower Drive, The Jubilee Garden

The Lower Drive is the start of the journey from lodge to house; halfway up it divides into two parallel paths. Your attention is caught in spring by the rhododendrons – the large-leaved, white-flowered *R. loderi*, a *R. vernicosum* hybrid cascading white, and several *R. arboreum* – that are one of Trengwainton's trademark plants.

There are mighty trees here too, including a *Ginkgo biloba,* known to survive for a thousand years or more and reputed to possess miraculous anti-ageing properties (an even better specimen is to be found in the Orchard).

The Jubilee Garden

Turn left behind the lodge into the garden created by Simon Bolitho in 1978 to commemorate the Queen's Silver Jubilee. The drama of the bold plantings spread out under the shadow of huge southern beeches and Monterey pines is enhanced by a sense of adventure as you follow the gentle, curving rise of the path. This is one of the few parts of the garden where architectural plants are consciously grouped together for dramatic effect.

Here are *Phormium tenax,* acanthus, yuccas and the first sighting of *Echium pininana,* a flamboyant giant that has self-seeded throughout the garden. These big players are linked by a carpet of geraniums and crinums, daylilies and hostas. Look out for the first of many superb magnolias: *M. campbellii* 'Kew's Surprise', with its rich-pink cup-and-saucer flowers. Another surprise is the laurel circle with a Wollemi pine, *Wollemia nobilis,* at its heart. Thought until 1994 to have been extinct for two million years, coniferous but not a pine, and curious rather than handsome, there's something distinctly ancient about it still.

The Tree Fern Glade,
William Walk

At first planted as individuals, bamboos and tree ferns start to crowd in along the path, building to a climax as a bamboo corridor leads into the next, and very different, garden – the gloriously cool and tranquil Tree Fern Glade. Groves of *Dicksonia antarctica* flank the little stream crossed by rustic bridges and assert their bulky bodies in the background, with native ferns acting as feathery legwarmers. Standing among the tall native trees that create the shady, moist conditions the tree ferns demand, rhododendrons chosen to flower for a long season lighten the darkness and the prevailing green.

William Walk

William Walk, the third of the garden lying off the Lower Drive, was created in 1982 and commemorates the birth of Prince William. Its start is marked by a stand of bamboos at the centre of a crossroads, and the path rises gently again in the dim light created by the canopy of native and exotic trees, softened by a covering of hydrangeas, hostas and epimediums. The stream reappears, and with it a sprinkling of moisture-lovers. As you turn sharp left over the final bridge, the contemplative mood is broken by a noisy little waterfall. You are about to break into the light of the Stream Garden.

A prehistoric plant
Tree ferns, like Wollemi pines, are rooted in antiquity. They have a strange and wonderful structure and habit of growth: their beautiful fronds emerge tightly coiled, like a necklace of ammonites, and their fibrous coconut trunks are actually formed from the thick mass of their roots, which expands as the plant ages. Keeping the trunks moist is the key to their (extremely slow-growing) survival.

Above left The greenery of the Tree Fern Glade

The Stream Garden,
The Meadow

E. H. W. Bolitho's major landscaping contribution to the garden occurred in 1926, when he opened up part of the stream that had previously been channelled through an underground culvert. It was later enlivened by little cascades.

Before Thomas Robins Bolitho's Long Drive was tarmacked by the National Trust in the 1960s, the streamside plants were regularly covered in white dust during dry spells. Now, dust-free, a broad strip of spring and early-summer colour belts up the stream as far as the eye can see, as kingcups, yellow and white skunk cabbages and rodgersias, mimulus and candelabra primulas jostle with euphorbias, crocosmias, astilbes, hemerocallis, hostas and ferns.

At the back, bridging the gap between the Long Drive and the Long Walk, woodland trees have been underplanted with spring and summer flowers. At mid-height are many rhododendrons interspersed with mimosas, blue and white hydrangeas, clumps of bamboos and grasses, trees and native ferns, Australasian shrubs and Asiatic magnolias. It's a dense and colourful tapestry that strengthens year on year.

The Meadow

The Meadow opposite, which acts as an important visual counterpoint to the flower-packed Stream Garden, is actually a mini-arboretum. An oak, a lime, a magnolia and two pines commemorate members of the royal family, and a collection of other fine ornamental trees includes *Ginkgo biloba, Metasequoia glyptostroboides, Cornus kousa* var. *chinensis* and *Rhododendron macabeanum. Rhododendron* 'Yellow Hammer' flowers obligingly in both spring and in autumn, when the spectacularly coloured leaves of *Cercidiphyllum japonicum* give off a toffee-apple scent as they fall. It's not all about living trees, however: at the back stands a charming Edwardian summer house.

Below The Stream Garden

Below left The Meadow in autumn

The Upper Pond and Bridge

At the top end of the Long Walk, E. H. W. Bolitho used the sheltered conditions to establish a holding nursery for some of the rarities he was beginning to amass. Several of the oldest rhododendrons here were bred at Trengwainton for the first time and given by him names like 'Fusilier' (see page 11) and 'Bombadier' that harked back to his army career.

During the five halcyon years he spent in India after 1910, he made two or more expeditions to Ladakh and the north, which fuelled his passion for rhododendrons. He was also (and remained throughout his life, as frequent game entries in his Trengwainton Garden Book show) a keen hunter and shooter; while on honeymoon in 1914 he took his bride into the bush in search of panthers. Though this pastime is rightly out of fashion and favour now, as a narrative, it is a charming period piece: 'This morning we were away at six thirty and I imagine had great good luck as right away in the jungle my little man found a big calf quite a year old which had only just been killed by a panther which was close by. After having put Aggie up a tree for safety, I advanced but "spots" had moved off: anyway tonight with the least bit of luck I ought to get a shot, but of course I'm not going to take A out.'

Reaching the curving wooden bridge opposite the small, duckweed-green pond fringed by tree ferns, and winding past new plantations and a dipping pond, you experience another of the sudden changes of mood that is such a feature of the garden as a whole: the switch from deep darkness into the promise of light.

Left Dappled shade on the bridge over the Upper Pond

The Terrace

The broad terrace walk at the top of the garden is the outdoor, fair-weather equivalent of the long galleries common in Jacobean country houses, where the company would meet to stroll, gossip and admire the pictures when bad weather could not tempt them into the garden. From the top floor they might admire the formal garden beneath the windows or the countryside beyond. Here at Trengwainton, perambulating visitors have a close-up view of a summer border and a panoramic view of fields and hedges stretching away to St Michael's Mount and the Lizard Peninsula.

Here too, Trengwainton does not entirely follow conventional garden-making rules. For a start, it's placed quite a long way from the house and stands aloof from it, separated by the house lawn and the shrubs and trees flanking the end of the Long Walk. An engraving on the front of the 1866 sales catalogue (see page 4) shows Price's handsome two-storey Regency house dominating its lawn; today the porticoed Victorian mansion complex (almost a town in miniature) is fronted by a belt of mature trees. The Terrace, which was laid out using granite blocks in the late 1890s, actually has a wider view than the house.

Right The toposcope on the terrace and views across Mounts Bay to The Lizard

The great storm that tore through the garden in January 1990 not only decimated the parallel shelterbelts of native trees heading down towards the sea, but also destroyed the row of *Quercus ilex* planted at the back of the Terrace. In their prime they were a magnificent sight, bending right over the broadwalk – as can be seen from the single specimen remaining near the entrance. The holm oaks have been replanted further back, behind a broad mixed border filled with a lively assortment of perennials, shrubs and tender exotics – a range of blue agapanthus, delicate-flowered *Parahebe perfoliata* and *Romneya coulteri*, daisy-flowered lampranthus and osteospermum, fleshy *Aloe arborescens* and flamboyant proteas, leucodendrons and callistemons. Flowering interest lasts from spring to autumn.

The erection of a pair of white-painted wooden summerhouses and the planting of a bold strip of agapanthus – blue to mark the edge, white to delineate the steps – have enhanced the formal character of this, the high point of the garden. Edward Bolitho has added his own modern imprint by commissioning from the St Buryan sculptor Joe Hemming an octagonal slate toposcope housed within a low, dense frame of *Ilex dimorphophylla*. It is beautifully carved, with pictorial clues highlighting significant aspects of Cornish or Bolitho history: Zennor and its mermaid, Geevor Mine with attendant shovel, the Lamb & Flag marking the family's tin-smelting mark, and a tin of pilchards making a wry reference to the family's fishing interests.

The Azalea Garden

As the name suggests, this is one of the places to make for in May, when the dark glades below the house lawn are coloured and scented by the blooms of a famous collection of fragrant azaleas. Their small leaves and dense shapes make for a pointilliste effect, tempered by a glossy group of '-ation' camellias, varieties with determinedly uplifting names such as 'Anticipation', 'Citation', 'Donation', 'Exaltation', 'Innovation', 'Inspiration', 'Jubilation' and 'Salutation'. The impact made by the sheer number of flowers and the massing of plants flowering simultaneously is quite breathtaking.

A turning-circle at the end of one of the rabbit-warren of paths sees two mighty dinosaurs, *Cryptomeria japonica* 'Elegans' and *Rhododendron arboreum* 'Cornish Red', locking horns. A colourful trail of laurels, orange-trunked myrtles and *Rhododendron* 'Polar Bear' flowering right at the end of the season in July leads down past the splendidly thick and entwined stems of the sweet-scented, lily-flowered *Rhododendron* 'Loderi King George' to the rear of the Upper Pond.

The Long Walk

Connecting the lodge to the house, this is the walk that mistook itself for a drive. History has it that in 1897 Thomas Robins Bolitho felt obliged to create a wider, parallel carriageway in a field on the east side of the old drive because of the number of accidents caused by drunken coachmen racing down the narrow track, which is alternately winding and enticingly, misleadingly straight.

This is the story you take with you if you follow the path down from the top to the bottom – from the house to the lodge. If you reverse direction, however, and walk gently upwards through the historic plantations, it is a different creature entirely – a place to dawdle and a welcome escape from midsummer sun or year-round rain. Rhododendrons and blue and white hydrangeas crowd in on either side, glowing white and blue in the half-shade of mature native trees – beech, sycamore and ash – that have been varied by more recently planted conifers and bamboos, such as the yellow-striped *Phyllostachys bambusoides* 'Castillion' and the black-stemmed *P. nigra*. The narrow stream trickles to one side, and through the clearings can be glimpsed the Long Drive and the wider garden.

At the junction of paths that beckon in several directions, cross over the stream and take the path straight ahead of you, where a tall brick barrier signals the western end of Price's extraordinary Walled Garden.

Far left **The Long Walk**

Left **The Azalea Garden**

The Camellia Walk

In 1926 an exciting horticultural event took place in the famous garden at Caerhays in east Cornwall – the first flowering of the cross between the tender, small-flowered *Camellia japonica* and *C. saluenensis,* discovered in Yunnan by George Forrest in 1918. It was a marriage made in heaven: the *C.* x *williamsii* hybrids, which proved to be hardy throughout the UK, with an attractively upright habit of growth and a very long flowering season, became almost the signature flower of Cornwall.

In 1939 E. H. W. Bolitho decided to plant a concentration of them as a walkway, separated by a narrow path, along the west wall of the Walled Garden, with the drama of their glossy dark leaves and boastful blooms brought out by the feathery foliage of *Sophora japonica* and *Lomatia ferruginea* in the background. In the north of Portugal there is a remarkable topiary garden, Casa do Campo: a series of outdoor rooms sculpted entirely out of camellias, many of them a century old and more. Trengwainton's Camellia Walk may be less ambitiously architectural, but in spring the dozens of bushes flowering white, rose and red is a similarly breathtaking sight.

Above left *Sophora japonica*

Above right *Lomatia ferruginea*

Right *Camellia* × *williamsii* 'Donation'

The Walled Garden

Trengwainton is essentially a long and linear garden. The exception is the strangely charismatic complex of walled gardens carved by Price out of farmland around 1815. Shaped like a huge lozenge divided into three longitudinal sections – the Lower Walled Garden (see over), the Kitchen Garden (pages 26–27) and the Orchard (pages 28–29) – it was set, in the Scottish tradition of kitchen gardens, a considerable distance from the house.

In order to protect crops and flowers from wind and frost, a curving granite wall, known as a Cornish hedge, was built to encircle the whole four acres. It was joined onto straight and beautifully crafted brick walls of Flemish bond, which run east-west and north-south to create ten small garden rooms: five in the rectangular Kitchen Garden in the middle and five in the Lower Walled Garden adjoining. As if this were not unusual enough, Sir Rose added on his west-facing cross-walls a series of sloping beds filled with soil. The concept was unique, the execution masterly.

Above left The view through to the Walled Garden

Cornish hedges

Cornish farmers have been building their stone 'hedges' for around 6,000 years. As wide as they are high, the core is always made of earth, with granite typically used as the facing in the west of the county, slate further east. They are all things to all species: vegetation sprouts through the cracks and bushes, encouraging plant species and wildlife, and bushes or trees grow along the top, used for coppicing. It has been estimated that a mile of healthy hedge might be host to some 300 plant species; Trengwainton's is 380 metres long.

The Lower Walled Garden

In its layout and planting, the Lower Walled Garden at the southern end has seen the most dramatic change of character and use. The growth of lichen, moss and tree ferns on the Cornish hedge at the southern end has given it a haunted atmosphere, and the huge, runaway old trees and understorey of self-seeded plants has turned them into a fascinating and sometimes bewildering place to explore.

It is likely that the five outdoor rooms that make up the Lower Walled Garden were used to house unusual ornamentals around 1875, long before E. H. W. Bolitho fixed on them as the perfect place for Alfred Creek to propagate his Kingdon-Ward specimens. These were then added to by marginally hardy rarities, experimented with and cultivated with the help of Creek's successor, G. W. Thomas. It would be invidious, and indeed impossible, to put a figure on the number of different plants; a conservative guess has put the number of different species in flower during the year at a staggering 800, with at least 150 species represented. One or two giants demand attention as you enter each garden in turn, but everywhere you look there are clumps and individuals to draw their fire.

The Veitchii Garden

The Veitchii Garden was cleared by E. H. W. Bolitho in 1937, a year after he had planted as a centrepiece a fast-growing and now-magnificent *Magnolia* 'Peter Veitch', peaking in April with a mass of white, pink-flushed flowers. Other fine trees – *Magnolia campbellii alba,* the unusual *Rehderodendron macrocarpum* from China and a towering *Metasequoia glyptostroboides* with an unusual twisted trunk, grown from seed in 1947 – also cast their shadows over the turf.

The Campbellii Garden

The adjoining garden has gained its name from another venerable magnolia, the Sikkim native *M. campbellii,* whose lovely pink cup-shaped flowers appear in February and March. An unusual invader is a red-tipped epiphyte, *Fascicularia bicolor,* perched among its branches. Two others, *Michelia doltsopa* and *Stewartia sinensis,* continue into summer, combining heavily scented white flowers, strong green foliage and rich brown bark. There are also fine specimens of *Kalmia latifolia* and *Cyathea medullaris.*

The Middle Walled Garden

The third enclosure, where a central path leads through a gate in the wall into the Kitchen Garden, is the airiest and potentially the prettiest, with relaxed groupings of grasses, herbaceous perennials and tender exotics scattered beneath fine specimens of eucryphia and enkianthus, *Magnolia mollicomata* and *M. sprengeri* var. *diva.*

The Fuschia Garden

Beyond are two gardens that are more specialised in character. The first is filled with a collection of fuchsias from South America and South Africa, centred on a huge, orange-barked

tree, *Fuchsia excorticata*. Plants range from the tiny *F. microphylla* and *F. procumbens* to a number of unusual tender varieties and an impressive climber, *F. coccinea*, that has scrambled to the top of a tall athrotaxis by the entrance to the adjoining Foliage Garden. But from spring through to autumn there are other long-flowering rarities that regularly catch visitors' eyes: *Iochroma australe* with its beautiful blue trumpets, *Tibouchina urvilleana,* the brilliant purple glory bush from Brazil, and *Coriaria terminalis* var. *xanthocarpa,* remarkable for its fleshy, translucent yellow fruit.

The Foliage Garden

This is the place where mature trees and shrubs distinguished by their bold leaves – architectural, strikingly patterned or arrestingly coloured – share the space with more recently planted tender foliage plants. The weirdly sculptural *Pseudopanax ferox* looks as if it has strayed from another planet; the yellow-green bower on the south wall opposite, rather inviting to look at but decidedly spiky to sit upon, was cut out of a large *Podocarpus acutifolius* in 1993. While *Dranunculus vulgaris* smells unpleasantly of rotting flesh when its flowers open in spring, the large stand of *Tetrapanax papyrifer,* grown for its massive lobed and furry leaves, puts off flowering until the start of winter.

Left The giant, multi-limbed torso of *Magnolia campbellii* in the garden that takes its name

The Kitchen Garden

It's been suggested, and it's too nice an idea to dismiss, that Price's rather eccentric religious beliefs inspired him to design the middle strip of the Walled Garden according to the dimensions of Noah's Ark – 300 cubits long x 50 cubits wide, that is 400 feet x 67 feet.

It is here that the four west-facing sloping beds, raised like giant cold frames filled with soil, are seen most clearly; in the Lower Walled Garden, smothered by plant growth, they are all but invisible. Their unique construction was reputedly inspired by the bitter 'year without summer' of 1816 that followed the eruption of the Indonesian volcano Mount Tambora. It worked: Price, and the Bolithos after him, succeeded in growing a wide range of flowers and early and tender vegetables and fruit to serve the culinary needs of the household. Nowadays the house, the café and the shop all claim a share.

Although the straight, raked gravel paths and clipped box edgings hark back to the discipline of the Victorian age, today the five gardens that make up the Kitchen Garden are thoroughly modern. At the far end is a community garden planted by groups of local primary school-children and community groups with verve and enthusiasm (and a fairly relaxed attitude to maintenance). Next to it a grassy square sprawls with pumpkins and nasturtiums, for little else will grow under the shade and leaf-drip and among the roots of a towering *Magnolia mollicomata*.

The central garden with its round dipping pond and golden yew is the most painterly space. A changing thicket of annuals stands tall and dense, and the slope is planted with neat, colourful rows of beetroots and 'saladings', interspersed with glowing heliotropes, cornflowers and pinks, all enjoying the improved light levels and free-draining soil. Then come the main vegetable plantings: row upon row interplanted with blocks of antirrhinums, asters and sweet Willliams, with cloches for forcing and pears and apples trained against the south-facing wall. The far garden has a sprinkling of the unusual – loquat, avocado, pomegranate and the Chilean guava *(Myrtus ugni)* – but it is mainly laid to grass: a place for children to enjoy and events to unroll.

Left The walled Kitchen Garden of revolutionary design

Above Victorian-style glass cloches

The Orchard

The large, open area to the north has always been planted as an orchard, but the well-tutored rows of fruit trees are interrupted by a 'Dig for Victory' allotment, a broad lawn and an avenue of palms. The wall of succulents sprouting from the Cornish hedge (see page 23) at the topmost end is an unusual take on the age-old tradition, planted by two Trengwainton gardeners with a passion for growing these spongy curiosities, which bask in the night-storage-heater warmth of the granite walls.

The head gardener's house, straddling the wall between the Orchard and the Kitchen Garden, is now a bookshop. A café with an inviting lawn beckons (accessible from the car park), and over the wall of succulents can be glimpsed the usual panoply of garden buildings: a chicken house, a bothy, a mushroom house and a rare Messenger greenhouse.

Bee aware

- There are around 60,000 bees in the average hive; Trengwainton has three known colonies, totalling some 180,000 bees.
- Of the 4,000 or so tonnes of honey produced in the UK each year, Trengwainton's colony yields 150lbs.
- Bees make different-flavoured honey from different flower varieties, so the close mixed planting of flowers and vegetables in the Kitchen Garden is a deliberate strategy. Pictured above is a bee on borage.
- Bee casualties at Trengwainton have followed the international trend. Numbers have been decimated as a result of adverse weather and infection by the mite *Varroa destructor*. An independent member of the British Beekeepers' Association gives advice and support, and is training Philip Griffiths and Gareth Wearne as beekeepers.

Right The restored bee house in the Orchard in June

Above The restored Messenger greenhouse

Head gardeners

At Levens Hall in Cumbria, there were 10 gardeners in over 300 years. While Trengwainton can't rival that record, most of the head gardeners since 1894 (when records began) served for over 12 years, and two – Alfred Creek (1904–34) and Peter Horder (1970–2001) – for over 30.

It was not all plain sailing. G. W. Thomas, who arrived in 1934, remembered an interesting conversation with his predecessor: 'I gathered from Mr Povey ... that Mrs Robins Bolitho was a bit of a "handful" when the occasion arose and that was why [he] did not stop long.' Her husband was clearly less of a handful: when he died in 1925, he left to 'my good gardener' the tidy sum of £500. The tradition was carried on by E. H. W. Bolitho, who bought Mr Thomas a smallholding on his retirement; a reciprocal gift of mistletoe arrived at Trengwainton every Christmas.

Mr Creek, however, who apparently accepted Mrs Robins 'as part of the job', could give as good as he got. Visiting the garden in 1948, two years before his death, he wrote: 'The group of *rhodo Guissonianum [Rhododendron griersonianum]* I raised about 3 dozen and planted them in a group in the Jubilee, it's a lovely colour but they have made a mistake by cutting it back like a common hedge, if I had seen the Colonel I would have told him they had made a great mistake.'

His successor, G. W. Thomas, remembered E. H. W. Bolitho with affection: 'I can honestly say that during my 14 years at Trengwainton, I was treated with the greatest respect, both by Mrs Bolitho, and the Colonel and there was

Left Trengwainton gardeners at the end of the 19th century

never any occasion for the mildest reproach.'
E. H. W. Bolitho himself valued Thomas as 'an educated gardener', but reserved special praise for Creek, whom he described as 'an outstanding man, he knew little of the book side of garden, but as a practical gardener he was unsurpassed in Cornwall'.

Thomas saw his main role as being 'to keep a succession of vegetables, and Fruit, and sowing dates etc', and indeed, as a child Edward Bolitho recalls vast quantities of fruit and vegetables being sent up to the house during his mother's day: 'Goodness knows what she did with them all.' Plants were also grown for sale, and sent as far afield as London. In George Hulbert's time, during the 1950s, early anemones, daffodils and hydrangea heads were boxed up for Covent Garden, while bamboo canes went to London Zoo to feed the pandas.

Peter Horder was head gardener at a particularly interesting time, overlapping with both Simon and Edward Bolitho, and overseeing the second and third decades of the National Trust's stewardship. Like Creek and Thomas before him, he experienced the excitement of experimenting with tender plants new to Trengwainton and the South West.

From the 1920s the Bolithos set great store by exhibiting, not only at the RHS in Vincent Square but also at local horticultural shows in Ludgvan, Falmouth, Newquay, Camborne and Penzance, where their head gardeners were in demand to act as judges.

When the National Trust took over in 1961, the head gardener's job changed dramatically. Although E. H. W. Bolitho had opened his garden (on Sunday 24 May 1931 he noted: 'I threw the grounds open to the public, conduct of people, hundreds came, was entirely satisfactory'), the long season of regular opening required a sea change in working practices. Ian Wright, head gardener from 2001 to 2010, restored the Kitchen Garden and introduced new vigour to the plant collection with the help of a bevy of volunteers. Now donning the mantle of head gardener is Philip Griffiths, who in addition to that role and the care of an historic plant collection, also has the task of managing a modern-day visitor attraction.

Above left **Alfred Creek with his wife Alice**

Below **Alfred's successor, G. W. Thomas**

Trengwainton Today

A top ten of Trengwainton highlights is nigh-on impossible to compile from such a varied collection, but here are a few that we think should not be missed.

1. *Fuchsia excorticata*
This is the largest fuchsia and can grow up to 15 metres. It is easily recognisable by its red peeling bark. The small pinky brown flowers are difficult to see, as they hang directly from the bare branches and have an unusual blue pollen. These are followed by dark purple berries, which, although they look poisonous, have a unique sweet flavour and are delicious raw or cooked.

2. *Embothrium coccineum* These magnificent bright red flowers are why this plant is also called the Chilean Firebush. It is rather tender, and only really suitable for a sheltered place in the milder areas of Britain.

3. *Impatiens tinctoria*
In spite of its huge size and exotic orchid-like appearance, this is actually a sort of busy Lizzie! It is worth pausing to smell it, as the fragrance is one of the sweetest in the garden, although quite elusive; it smells strongest on a warm damp evening. From the uplands of central Africa, it is best suited to a temperate climate, although it will survive quite heavy frosts.

4. *Fascicularia bicolor* subsp. *bicolor*
This bromeliad – the same family as the pineapple – was

introduced to Europe from Chile in 1851. In autumn, the inner leaves turn bright red, just as the rosette of deep blue flowers opens up to reveal yellow stamens. The plant eventually makes a large mound of rosettes.

5. *Eucryphia*

These southern-hemisphere plants arrived in the UK as early as 1820. There are many champion trees in Cornish gardens where, in the mild climate, they have achieved sizes of 20 metres or more. The flowers are produced in autumn, individually small but showy and sweet-scented.

6. *Agapanthus*

The first plants were brought back from South Africa by Dutch settlers, with the first ones reaching England as long ago as 1687. The name comes from the Greek *agape* (love) and *anthos* (flower), hence the name 'flower of love', although they are commonly known as African Lily or Lily of the Nile. They are relatively easy to grow – good soil and lots of sun are their only requirements. They come in white as well as every possible shade of blue, and recently there has been a race to breed a pink one.

7. *Davidia involucrata*

Named after a French missionary, Abbé Armand David, sent to Peking in 1862 to teach science to children. To illustrate his lessons, he collected local plant and animal specimens (he is credited with introducing the first panda bear to the West). Although he sent back the first description of this tree, the first specimen was brought to England in 1901 by the famous plant hunter E. H. Wilson.

8. *Echium pininana*

These enormous plants, native to the Canary Islands, are actually only two or three years old. They show little more than a small leaf rosette in their first year, but eventually produce a flower spike, up to four metres high, with a mass of leaves and small but beautiful sky-blue flowers. Echiums like a warm spot that receives sun from different angles. They are only half-hardy, but they self-seed so readily that there always seems to be the odd survivor.

9. *Clerodendrum trichotomum* var. *fargesii*

This plant has abundant pink buds, opening to beautiful starry white flowers with a fabulous scent. These are followed by eye-catching metallic blue berries, and the leaves show good autumn colour. It is hardy and seems to thrive in any soil or situation; all it needs is a little sunshine. Please plant one – it deserves to be much more widely grown!

10. *Crinodendron hookerianum*

Introduced from Chile in 1848, this plant has beautiful crimson lantern-like flowers. The name comes from the Greek *krinon* (lily) and *dendron* (tree), although anything that looks less like a lily-tree would be hard to imagine.

Rhododendron rescue

In the past, rhododendrons were grown thickly throughout the garden at Trengwainton. This can make them vulnerable to disease, and so the National Trust has taken out a horticultural insurance policy in the shape of micropropagation. The building up of a disease-free bank of prized or vulnerable species by means of tissue culture has been going on in America (driven, ironically enough, by the tobacco industry) since the late 1930s. However, the most potent driver as far as our own Gulf Stream counties are concerned has been the devastating effects of *Phytophthora ramorum*. This disease used to be known as 'sudden oak death' but has now been renamed 'rhododendron decline'.

The tell-tale signs of drooping new growth first appeared in 2004 on rhododendrons at Trengwainton and Heligan, travelling, it was thought, on camellias from Asia via Holland. When Defra confirmed this phytophthora as a disease new to the UK, it was the horticultural equivalent of BSE. Panic measures were taken to strip out contaminated plants, and a disease-free replacement programme took shape. Duchy College Rosewarne, operating from a post-war Ministry of Agriculture site near Camborne, was already working on conserving old rhododendron species at Heligan. In EU terms, Cornwall was already considered in need of support, and this new threat to her tourist industry and the possible long-term loss of heritage material prompted the award of European funding. The college became the only UK laboratory licensed to micropropagate potentially infected plant material.

It is a straightforward, if time-consuming and therefore costly, propagation method, with a success rate of something like 90 per cent. As Ros Smith, Laboratory Manager at Duchy College, explains, it is a manipulation of nature: 'In effect the plant is being persuaded to change its mind from being in flowering mode to shooting mode.' Flower buds (the earlier in their development the better) are harvested and sterilised with diluted bleach, first removing their scale leaves, as these have been found to contain a high level of contamination. Individual florets are then soaked in plant growth hormones and placed in pots of agar gel. Lined up in serried ranks in a sterile environment under fluorescent tube lighting for 16 hours a day at 22°C, they start to produce shoots from the base. When the shoots are quite big, they are cut off and put into a fresh lot of gel made to a different formula. The final stages are familiar to gardeners: treated with rooting gel, placed in peat-based compost, hardened off in a mist house, and they are then put out in their final positions in the garden.

Using this method, not only can thousands of disease-free plants be created at any one time, but they become rejuvenated; useful for cutting material and rooting more easily than the originals. The college works with its clients, including the National Trust, on a conservation rather than a commercial basis, but an increasing range of popular plants – camellias and viburnums, primulas and orchids – is now being offered for sale to individuals.

Four Trengwainton rhododendrons grown by E. H. W. Bolitho have been given the treatment: *R. macabeanum* (the creamy yellow species brought back by Frank Kingdon-Ward); 'Morvah' (a cross between *R. elliottii* and *R. wattii*, named for the village in the Penwith peninsula made famous by the centuries-old annual fair, which was denounced by its priest in the late 19th century for the drunken and promiscuous behaviour of 'disorderly persons of every description'); *R.* 'Creek's Cross' commemorating Trengwainton's most famous head gardener, Alfred Creek; and the ravishing pale pink double 'Johnnie Johnston'.

Opposite A rhododendron showing signs of the fungal disease *Phytophthora ramorum*

Above left Cultures in the growth room

Below left Single divisions removed from shoots

Above The ravishing *R.* 'Johnnie Johnston' is one of the four rhododendrons being microprogated at Trengwainton

A tale of three dynasties

Trengwainton's character was formed by two powerful dynasties. It is now being influenced by a third: the general public. In the 1970s, 4,000 visitors came to the garden; now there are some 60,000, and they are changing the form and focus of the place.

The plant collections were formerly the whole *raison d'être* of the garden. The Terrace, once merely a pleasant detour for houseguests, is now one of its highpoints and as such enhanced by sculpture and planting. Similarly, the Kitchen Garden and Orchard were jobbing areas: now they are designed for visitors to explore and interact with. The shop, plant sales, bookshop and café have further widened the scope of the garden.

Trengwainton is of course challenged by other outside forces. Climate change, altering as it does weather patterns and flowering times, has been met by changes to established horticultural practice. A multiplication of diseases has led to collaborative micropropagation projects.

Certain key plant collections are nearing the end of their lives and must be replenished, which gives the chance to experiment with new species and varieties. And while the sprouting of wind turbines and solar panels may be slowing down, important vistas are under constant threat from house-building programmes, making a rolling programme of screens as well as shelterbelts a permanent priority.

Trengwainton has always been a place of experimentation, and that innovation has been recognised by the most august horticultural societies. Now visitors in their thousands come to admire this award-winning garden. The new challenge, then, is to continue to inspire and excite. Garden visitors, like policeman, are getting younger, and Cornwall is suddenly a much trendier place to be. Trengwainton, with the aim of staying part of that trend, will continue to innovate.

Above The Kitchen Garden in full bloom

Left Trengwainton hopes to attract a variety of visitors

Below Younger visitors at the front door of Trengwainton's Nanceglos House, available as a holiday let